Strands

Strands

By Marianne Barber

Published by Ponsanooth 2008

Copyright © 2008
Marianne Barber

The right of Marianne Barber to be identified as the author of this work has been asserted by her in accordance with the Copyright, Designs and Patents Act 1988.

All Rights Reserved
No reproduction, copy or transmission of this publication may be made without written permission. No paragraph of this publication may be reproduced, copied or transmitted save with the written permission or in accordance with the provisions of the Copyright Act 1956 (as amended).

ISBN 978-0-9555987-0-8

Reprinted in 2010

Printed and bound in Great Britain by:
Limited Editions, Remus House, Coltsfoot Drive
Woodston, Peterborough PE2 9JX

Marianne Barber was born in Sheffield and has lived in Cheshire, Surrey and Sussex. She studied at Kingston University as a mature student and obtained a BA (Hons) in English and the History of Ideas in 1998. She has three children and ten grandchildren. Marianne was a prizewinner in Waterstone's Kingston University Bookshop Poetry Competition in 2000 and has read her poetry at a number of arts venues throughout Surrey and Sussex.

**In remembrance of my mother,
Marian Betty Barber
1915-1994**

Acknowledgements

Acknowledgements are due to the editors of the following publications in which some of these poems, or versions of them, first appeared: *Hear My Voice* (Napier Nationwide, 1996); *The Lady*, November-December 1996; *Rumours* Magazine, May, June and October 1997; Short *Cuts Poetry: Kingston Readers' Festival Poetry Competition 2004 (Borders Bookshop, 2004)*; *The Omnibus Anthology: Haiku and Senryu*, comp. Fred Schofield (Hub, 2001); Time Haiku No 13 Spring 2001; This is *My Voice 2000*, ed. Gerald Baker, Colin Bloxham and Anne Rowe (Kingston Cultural Services/ Waterstones, 1999); This is *My Voice 2000*, ed. Gerald Baker, Colin Bloxham and Anne Rowe (Kingston Heritage Arts & Tourism Services/Waterstones, 2000) and *Yours Magazine*, issue 6, June 2001.

CONTENTS

High Time	1
After the Rain	2
Love	3
Moonhoney	4
Strandline	5
Slanting Rain	6
The Scarf	7
Ladies First	8
Compressed Women	9
The Case of Living	10
Titled Undecided	12
Pen Names	13
The Birth of Aphrodite	14
The Bored Gondolier	15
Cinderella City	16
Unlucky for Some	17
In Memorandum	18
Mum's Floorcloth	19
The Explanation	20
Childhood Ritual	21
In Remembrance of Marian Betty Barber 1915-1994	23
Messages	25
The Last Strand	26
School of Souls	27
Industrial Meadows	28
Windmill Girls	29
Inspiration	30
Knowledge	31
Waiting for Symbols	32
The Phone Spider	33
Sycamore Injuns	34
The Predicament of Pom-Pom Dhalia	35
The Fast Lane	36
Damsels of Distinction	37
Haiku	38
Optimism	39

High Time

The ducks bob on the river –
and orange clad canoeists.
Life goes by while I watch
and wait for the right time,
the right tide, to paddle my canoe.

All the world is on the move;
everyone drives their cars, except me;
everyone drives their power externally,
but I drive inwardly, on unleaded petrol
called intuition, waiting for the choke
to ignite, enabling me to write,
put down new roots, build a home and
plant a garden.

Every other night a futile exercise –
a finger points in the atlas,
searching for inspiration, an
intuitive place to reside.

Horizon, sparkle on the sea.
Reality, appear for me, waiting
to unearth the cockle shell
after the tide.

After the Rain

After the rain
we visited abandoned allotments,
looking for orphaned seedlings
to plant in the garden.

We found lupin leaves
balancing scales of crystal,
whose beads fell like quicksilver
from inverted umbrellas.

Love

It first comes as an ignition
of childhood contentment;
warm and comfortable like the feel
of hands in a silky pocket.

It looks and smells like
golden brown wallflowers.
Its texture is orange yellow nasturtiums.
Its base note is the sap of a snapdragon.

Then hearts bleed in dicentra's
feathered foliage.
The silver black moon tide
tugs away from easing shore.

Lastly it springs like a persistent weed
leaving its shadow
in a shaft of sunlight
on the garden wall.

Moonhoney

You carried the cases,
I carried my straw hat with lilac ribbon.
We strolled and shopped in the town –
I bought a cape,
you full of admiration.

The beds were single,
not being room enough for two
I withdrew, clasping the bedcover.
'Can I have my sheet back please?'
was your naked request.

Never-ending giggles and guffaws followed.
Recollecting –
it was the best holiday I've ever had.
We weren't married of course:
it was just moonhoney.

Strandline

Ours is not a love knot,
but a rope, and we are each
frayed ends held by tenuous strands,
some coarse, some fine, some brittle;
made by time and circumstance;
pulled without surrender.

Ours is not a love knot,
but a silken skein of embroidery
running blood red on open cracks
of dried tear paths.

Ours is not a love knot,
but a silvery line
where sea meets sand,
meeting and parting
before a beckoning tide.

Slanting Rain

You went to the sun
and left me in dark December;
'See you soon,' you said –
'I'll be too busy to notice,' said I.

And now surviving and vulnerable,
like a fly on a wet window pane
opaque with condensation,
I only see the slanting rain.

The Scarf

I had a beautiful warm Peruvian coloured scarf,
everyone admired it.
It looked good with my mac and coats.
My lover wanted to exchange it for his.
I didn't really want to
but he said his scarf of beige and brown matched my coat.

I parted with my scarf and lover.
The brown scarf remains stuffed in my wardrobe
and now I have a new lover.
He bought me a scarf of Indian silk, orange and brown.
I don't know whether to throw the beige brown scarf away
or give it to my new lover.
But I'd have to tell him where it came from,
and I don't think he'd like to wear it then.

Ladies First

My pillars are not of stone or marble
nor decorated with caryatids or cast iron figures,
but soft and strong like tissue paper,
unable to tear easily.

Not always visible but ever present,
their roles interchange between reliance and support.
Sometimes the pillars vibrate with party gossip,
at other moments revolve into listening posts.

These pillars have feminine names –
How could we live amongst men
without our women friends'
empathy and advice?

Compressed Women

Women are like
compressed Chinese paper flowers
which open in water.

Women are like travellers
on a Hiroshige print.

Women are like compressed
dates in a slab;
layers of leaves fermenting.

But when decompression comes,
women are images of spectrum
transformed from dust
circling in shafts of sunlight
in a quiet room.

The Case of Living

'All parties in the case of 'Living' go to Court 8.'
'Be upstanding in court.'
'Will the defendants please stand.
Are you Adam?
Are you Eve?
Sit down please.'

'Jury in court.'
'Eve you are accused of sleeping,
Adam, of eating.
How do you plead?'
'Not guilty.'
'Not guilty.'

I represent the case for the Prosecution
and we say, Eve was a temptress,
responsible for Adam's fall.
What do you say, Eve?'
'I say, not at all –
I was sharing the apple which
fell off the tree –
a poisoned green apple the
snake gave to me.
This wriggly green snake
slithered beside me in bed,
stung me with venom from his
snakey green head. Unconscious,
I lay beside Adam, who woke
with a bite of the apple
stuck in his throat.

'Stand in the witness box, Adam.'
'Sir, I was hungry and wanted a taste of sin.
I took a bite and the apple slipped in –
golden delicious weren't ripe just then.'

'I give you credit for previous good character.
Your sentence will be partners in life,
joined together in matrimony, named man and wife.
Discharge for you both in the case of giving,
for the sorrows of life can't escape trial of 'Living'.

Title Undecided

I can't decide, she said,
whether I want brown or white bread;
whether I take one lump or two;
I can't decide, she said.

I can't decide, she said,
which cake to choose to eat today;
chocolate, walnut, coffee or caraway;
I can't decide, she said.

I can't decide she said,
as she sailed under the wishing bridge,
which wish to choose, before – too late –
the boat had sailed under the gate.
I can't decide, she said.

I can't decide, she said,
which man to choose, thin or fat,
tall or short, this or that,
so just for now, I'll milk the cow
and eat my bread and drink my tea and
have my cake and eat it!

Pen Names

'That green pen
is always pushing in.
He's not really popular,
but he's always there, ready,
when we are having a quiet snooze
underneath the envelopes or
nestling with the pencils.
He never dries up while we strive
to keep our ink flowing.
Always seen in the right places
in the jam jar with blunt pencils and
worn out pens, he sticks himself upright
I think he's seeing a lot of that red pen –
they say plumes of a feather flock together,
but I say, red and green should never be seen.'

'There's a quill in my background.
My family had a silver inkstand,
and when I was bought I lay in a beautiful
velvet case.'

'I really do think your ink's lovely.
What's the name?'
'Brilliant blue.'
'I bet you make a lovely blot.'

'I like your ink.
What's its name?'
'Ebony black'.
You make nice strokes,
such fine neat lines,
with such flourish.'

'You're making me go all blotchy.
Stop it.'
'Alright - give us a kiss.'

The Birth of Aphrodite

With volcanic force
from frothy waters
where Uranus' sperm
had lain long
on the ocean,
Aphrodite
burst, showering high
a chasm of sea jewels;
body and skin new and
white as a just opened
water lily,
eyes half closed like a
fulfilled lover.

The Bored Gondolier

Unsmiling, unhatted, chewing gum,
the gondolier thrusts his way through canals,
steering against stone walls with trainers.

Unserenaded,
passive passengers,
view scenery unlit by enthusiasm or smile.

Ignoring his audience,
the gondolier shouts and
smiles to fellow Venetians.

No extras given;
the hand stretched out at jetty
points to upturned hat.

Six more passengers;
the gondolier pushes off,
replacing his mask.

Cinderella City

Step inside for a
ride in my gondola;
I'll show you bridges
like you've never seen –
fit for a queen to
pass under.

Peer through your
mask in streets of
Venetian pink glass;

Murano beads to tease,
crepe de chine to screen
Pierrot and Pantaloon.

Love lurks and Harlequin,
see him, catch him, dressed
in party clothes, darting
in and out of shadows.

Quick, before the magic fades
come with me in cavalcade;
ride on vanished unicorn,
carnival till dawn;
dance, silhouette the moon,
lighting on lagoon.

How much this magic trip
on your gondola black ship,
wearing your beribboned hat;
how much for that?

For two of us?
I see –

Let's go and have a
cup of tea and take the
River Bus.

Unlucky for Some

She was seventy seven, my mum,
sinking into black depression
and then I visited,
plucked her eyebrows and chin,
filed and varnished her nails,
put her earrings back in,
sang a song in the kitchen.
She called – sing it again.

In Memorandum

Mum was a bit like Hylda Baker –
always getting her words mixed up.
Flamber Gascoigne used to compere
University Challenge.

December 17th, my mother's birthday;
the day we put up Christmas decorations.
According to custom I lit the candle her grandson
brought back from Mont san Miquel.

I tried to find her voice through old tapes
rescued from the flat clearance.
In the background of Max Bygraves' Christmas songs
I heard the tinkle of tea-cups and whispered voices.
Was it her cough, did she say,
'Thank you Mrs Bennett very much?'

She was always thanking people.
In my ignorance, I sometimes felt embarrassed.
I'm trying to think more interlectrically,
see things clearly – though Kant says
we cannot see the real world, only the
phenomenal world of appearance;
the real world is not visible.

We can glimpse it occasionally.
I know Keats did when I read 'Ode to a
Nightingale,' and my mother did in her imagination.
A lot of words were kept in.
Perhaps that is why some
became jumbled on the way out.

Mum's Floorcloth

Old vests used as floor cloths
aren't seen anymore,
but one turned up yesterday
at my door, it was me.

Grey, moth-eaten, soggy, gritty eyed,
I hung myself on the bucket to dry
like seaweed and emerged stiff and
crinkly, with bits of sand stuck to me.

I put myself in a bath to refloat,
painted and powdered and
put on my coat –

Like a sprinkling of vim on a china
teacup, descended the stairs with
my chin up, forgetting the hem of
my coat was undone.

My spirits were lifted as I picked
myself up and saw Mrs. Bennett, who
said 'hello duck'. She knelt on
the floor, with her magic bucket

and an old floor cloth, like mum's,
twisted and shook.
There's nothing like old vests
for cleaning up muck.

The Explanation

One night I was afraid.
The wind was in a rage.
Scared, I called you
to my bed and you said –
'God has to send the
wind to make the windmills
go round. Then from
Holland it crosses the
South Seas and becomes
a gentle breeze; pretend
you are lying on the sand' –
and I would fall asleep.

Childhood Ritual

Night night, she said.
Night night, I said.
Night night,
Night night,
Night night.

And so it went on till my mother
reached the foot of the stairs;
stairs which I had fallen down often,
usually carrying something unwieldy,
like a giant jigsaw or my brother's
Meccano set.

Stairs which were swept with a stiff
brush on the middle carpet, knocking
the stair-rods and sides, creating a
special dusty staircase smell.

When we were naughty, sitting on the
bottom of the stairs was our punishment.
At school, there was a golden staircase –
a picture of a staircase to heaven.
with each penny given to the special cause,
your name would ascend one more step.

I reached heaven,
which surprised me because
I had been off school, ill with earache.

It's not so easy to get to heaven now –
inflation, more temptation, more
swear words about.
Impulsive steps are broken. Hesitation comes
before the next step is taken.
I'm climbing up the stairs again,
I hope I don't fall down.

Night night, I said.
Night night, she said.
The role reverses.
She in heavenly bed,
me, at the foot of the stairs.

In Remembrance of Marian Betty Barber 1915-1994

Little Betty Barber,
sent away to school;
for she had no father,
and that was then the rule.

Her mother she knew as her aunt,
because of the disgrace;
but little Betty Barber
had such a pretty face.

Holidays weren't spent at home
while grandfather was alive.
She said she wasn't wanted
and became an early bride.

A love match it really wasn't;
her beau, the butchers boy,
thought he was on to a good thing,
a rich heiress, his ploy.

Little Betty Barber,
kept a sweetie shop,
gave away the chocolates – for
one penny, children got a lot.

Little Betty Barber,
invented magic things;
fairy dewdrop under pillows and
mother Easter after spring.

She explained to frightened children,
fearful of the gales –
God has to send the wind to
blow the windmills' sails.

Little Betty Barber,
now has gone to rest;
she didn't always see the light,
but always did her best.

We scatter her ashes,
her spirit living still,
comforts as we stand on
this Rivelin Valley hill;
a most beautiful place,
in which to remember
Betty Barber's pretty face.

Messages

I received your messages mum.
Some sceptics would believe otherwise,
but I knew when the luggage label from
your case fluttered, you were waving me
goodbye.

Soon after, you sent another message on
the train – a heavenly sunset.
On the bus, I watched through the window
as you blew kisses from the cross-beams
of street lamps and cars.
Everywhere I looked, lights shined
your affection.

In my bed I cried for a sign from you again,
and the dead carnation on the windowsill
stirred, its thin leaves soothingly patted
the draughty air.

The Last Strand

I'd often wished I'd saved
some of her strong, silvery hair.
I brought her carpet sweeper
into use, and emptied
the folds of felted dust.
It was there –
woven as woollen tweed
like fossils in a layer.

Carefully gathering
a few strands,
I lay them down
on blue paper,
folded neatly,
like her.

School of Souls

When I was small
I thought a soul
had a shape like an
elongated inverted triangle.

This shape would fit
easily and comfortably
beneath my chest,
behind my blazer pocket.

Eating my cod fish portion
I recall these thoughts.
They say the eye is the
mirror of the soul and
birds, like God, have
an aerial view.

Industrial Meadows

When factories fell and died,
machines no longer whirred and burred,
site cleared and flattened,
something happened.

Sunlight shone on factory floor,
unhindered by window and door;
a brick wall sunbathed in the afternoon,
and children played.

Rosebay willow herb grew,
blue butterflies flew,
wasps moved into the warm brick wall
and whirred with bird.

In late afternoon, through
haze of sun when end of shift
was sounded, still here tread the
working dead, laughter and cries
since ended.

Windmill Girls

I chose my sister,
she was younger but
taller than me.
Her name was nearly the same as mine;
she invited me to tea.

We played 'tea-sets',
painted through stencils,
licked gummed paper shapes
tried on hats;
pretended a dapple grey mare
would carry us off, away from
our third storey flats.

We galloped along at the seaside;
trailed our spades in the sand;
gingerly walked in the rock pools,
me holding my big sister's hand.

I bought windmills and flags
for our castles,
fish and chips on the prom,
for my sister who is fifty three
and me aged sixty one.

Inspiration

Inspiration – no light,
I got poem to write.
I shop.
Inspiration, no sweat,
yea boys, no sweat.

Cosmetics, sure thing,
counterchicks, ring a ding ding.
Lipstick, Ferrari red;
too fast to wear in bed.
Inspiration, no sweat,
yea boys, no sweat.

Gossamer pink, a shade too fey.
I need something to wear today –
hot – to give away.
Orange flame, sure thing
flaming June, a ring a ding ding.
Inspiration, no sweat.
yea boys, no sweat.

Pouting pink, in your face, too strong,
little coy, little wrong.
Fuchsia pink, guess will kiss just fine.
I'll put it in my bag when I go to dine.
Inspiration, sure thing,
yea yea, ring ding.

Knowledge

I am small in stature
and not fat;
therefore, I cannot take in
too much knowledge at once.

I take in a bit at a time
and shake it down by getting up,
walking about and drinking tea.

As a result, I know a little of
everything, but not the complete
story, it simply won't all fit.

Sometimes I try to fit too
much in my head and it goes in
one ear and out the other.

At exam time it is very difficult.
I have to intersperse study with
telephone calls to cope with
word surplus.

Knowledge is like a basket of fruit;
some unripe, some mouldy,
only a few pieces easy to digest.

Waiting for Symbols

Symbols are powerful and mysterious
- a forecast, transparent yet assuming an edifice.

In France, the Epiphany cake –
La Galette des Rois –
inside the symbol of good fortune –
slices are taken – who is lucky?

The young lady – an aspiring actress
gives the porcelain figure to another,
yet the year is already hers:
the symbol spent and powerless.

Standing at the back of the orchestra
the alert cymbalist and drummer listen for their cue
and demonstrate
we always wait for symbols.

The Phone Spider

Seated at my circular table
I talk on the telephone
weaving the flex, like a spider
doing a courtship dance.

Hand attached to receiver
I spin my web moving my
body in all directions.

I kneel on the chair,
lean forward, hanging my face
inches from the tablecloth.

Sideways, I twist my legs,
perching on a further chair and
find myself lying backward,
facing the ceiling.

I cannot replace the receiver,
it is tangled in sticky spider thread.

Sycamore Injuns

Proudly flying leaf feathers,
tossing their feathered main,
backward, forward and sideways
to an east wind's refrain.

Branches of tall warriors,
Navajo or Sioux,
stretch to see horizons,
smoke messages in view.

Big Chief Thundercloud
encircles pow-wow's trance;
agitates and shudders to
perform his rain dance.

Looking through the curtains,
them injuns notice me;
and change as fast as rapids
into a sycamore tree.

The Predicament of Pom-Pom Dahlia

An earwig listening in the dahlias,
heard a pom-pom seldom failures
to be a little tiddly.

The petals, said the nettles,
are too loud for copper kettles to
decorate the settle in the tiddly-pom.

More earwigs listened in,
crawling out to hear the din and
shaved the prickly nettle's chin.

The dahlias bent and swayed,
drunk with summer's day,
drowsy nettles lost their sting
for the butterfly on wing.

Earwigs chose to snooze
on that sunny afternoon.
All quiet at three;
babes on mother's knee,
then the band came playing –

Tiddly,
Tiddly pom,
Tiddly pom pom
Pom pom
Tiddly.

The Fast Lane

The rain
in Spain
comes down
the drain,
but in
the main
the window-pane.

Some people say
that I'm insane,
but really I'm
a little vein,
trickling down
the window-pane,
zooming like an aeroplane,
for reasons that
I can't explain;
unless of course
I were a train
a main line train,
that in the rain,
comes through the tunnel
like a drain –
in Spain.

Damsels of Distinction***

Virtuous virgins,
pleasing to taste;
adore reputation,
don't marry in haste.

Ladies in waiting,
with almondy eyes,
melting like butter
beneath Richmond skies.

Dusted with sugar,
presented with tea,
the maids lost their honour,
while Henry took three.

***Maids of Honour cakes – invented by a baker in Richmond near Henry VIIIs Palace, named after the ladies-in-waiting.

Haiku

Earthy leafed fragrance
yellow chrysanthemum
a silent Sunday

Ruby berries drop –
Japanese setting sun
on Autumn rowan

Optimism

Would look like a lighthouse swishing its beam
Textured like hand sewn bespoke tailor's seam
Sound like the ding of a conductor's bell
Be fiery and orange like Lucifer's hell
Taste like the burst of Bacchus's grape
Feel like a lover's kiss received on your nape
Smell like cooked beetroot in a greengrocer's shop
Feel like a skip, a jump and a hop.
If could speak it would say, 'Never tomorrow –
Time passes so quick there is no time for sorrow.'